MY SIGHT WORD WORK BOOK & READER LEVEL 1

Welcome to the **My Sight Word Workbook & Reader** series. This is a unique book in which the focus is on developing students sight word recognition skills. The tracing and reading of the sight words and the many activities and tests are designed to allow students to successfully master sight word recognition. Knowledge of sight words will enable students to read fluently. It is important to note that sight words make up over **70%** of all words found in most reading material that students will encounter. Without sight word knowledge, reading will not progress as it should. The activities in this text are designed to enhance the teaching and learning process for teachers and students. It is the author's wish that this text will be productive and enjoyable.

This workbook belongs to:

SELLINGTON PUBLISHERS
DREAM BIG DREAM BOOKS

THIS SIGHT WORD BOOK SERIES (1-3 & THE COMPLETE VOLUME) IS PUBLISHED AND OWNED BY SELLINGTON PUBLISHERS.

My Sight Word Workbook and Reader : Level 1, Book 2 Text Copyright © 2018 by Jacqueline Mitchell.
Cover art and Interior illustrations Copyright © 2018 by Pete McDaniel.

All Rights Reserved. No part of this book may be reproduced in any form or by any electronic or mechanical means including information storage and retrieval systems, without permission in writing from the author. The only exception is by a reviewer, who may quote short excerpts in a review.

First Edition

ISBN 978-1-7322038-4-6

MY SIGHT WORD

WORKBOOK & READER

LEVEL 1 • BOOK 2

JACQUELINE MITCHELL WITH
ILLUSTRATIONS BY PETE MCDANIEL

Trace the word "go". Say the word "go" aloud.

go go go go go

In each sentence below, trace the word: "we".

I will go home now.

How will you go?

I will go by bus.

I will go by train.

I will go on a taxi.

No! I will not go.

Write your own sentence using the word: go.

Read the sentences below. Circle the word "go" in each sentence. Colour the picture below.

I will go home now.
How will you go?
I will go by bus.
I will go by train.
I will go on a taxi.
No! I will not go.

Trace the word "for". Say the word "for" aloud.

for for for for for for for

In each sentence below, trace the word: "**for**".

A is for apple and astronaut.

B is for bat and ball.

C is for cat and car.

D is for dog and duck.

E is for egg and eye.

F is for farmer and flower.

Write your own sentence using the word: **for**.

Read the sentences below. Circle the word "for" in each sentence. Colour the picture below.

A is for apple and astronaut.
B is for bat and ball.
C is for cat and car.
D is for dog and duck.
E is for egg and eye.
F is for farmer and flower.

Trace the word "big". Say the word "big" aloud.

big big big big big

In each sentence below, trace the word: "big".

The cat is big.

The big cat is on the mat.

The big cat is drinking milk.

The big cat can run.

The big cat can jump.

See the big cat run and play.

Write your own sentence using the word: big.

Read the sentences below. Circle the word "**big**" in each sentence. Colour the picture below.

The cat is big.
The big cat is on the mat.
The big cat is drinking milk.
The big cat can run.
The big cat can jump.
See the big cat run and play.

Trace the word "can". Say the word "can" aloud.

can can can can can

In each sentence below, trace the word: "**can**".

I can kick the ball.

I can make my bed.

Can you see the fish?

Yes. I can see the fish.

The horse can jump.

The birds can fly.

Write your own sentence using the word: **can**.

Read the sentences below. Circle the word "can" in each sentence. Colour the picture below.

I can kick the ball.
I can make my bed.
Can you see the fish?
Yes. I can see the fish.
The horse can jump.
The birds can fly.

Trace the word "not". Say the word "not" aloud.

not not not not not

In each sentence below, trace the word: **"not"**.

I was not at home.

I did not see you at the zoo.

Did I not tell you to be quiet?

We are not afraid of the lion.

Not all of the animals are scary.

Write your own sentence using the word: **not**.

Read the sentences below. Circle the word "**not**" in each sentence.

I was not at home.
I did not see you at the zoo.
Did I not tell you to be quiet?
We are not afraid of the lion.
Not all of the animals are scary.

Trace the word "one". Say the word "one" aloud.

one one one one one

In each sentence below, trace the word: "**one**".

One day I went for a walk.

I found one egg.

The one egg was in a nest.

One big egg, in a nest.

I had one egg for breakfast.

The hen only laid one egg.

Write your own sentence using the word: **one**.

Read the sentences below. Circle the word "one" in each sentence. Colour the picture below.

One day I went for a walk.
I found one egg.
The one egg was in a nest.
One big egg, in a nest.
I had one egg for breakfast.
The hen only laid one egg.

Trace the word "red". Say the word "red" aloud.

red red red red red

In each sentence below, trace the word: "**red**".

The red hen is in the barn.

The red barn is on the farm.

Farmer Joe grows red potatoes.

He has a red pony.

The red pony likes to gallop.

Write your own sentence using the word: **red**.

Read the sentences below. Circle the word "red" in each sentence.

The red hen is in the barn.
The red barn is on the farm.
Farmer Joe grows red potatoes.
He has a red pony.
The red pony likes to gallop.

Trace the word "run". Say the word "run" aloud.

run run run run run

 In each sentence below, trace the word: "**run**".

We like to run and play.

We run to catch the ball.

We run and kick the ball.

It is fun to run and play.

When we run we get tired.

We have fun when we run.

 Write your own sentence using the word: **run**.

Read the sentences below. Circle the word "run" in each sentence. Colour the picture below.

We like to run and play.
We run to catch the ball.
We run and kick the ball.
It is fun to run and play.
When we run we get tired.
We have fun when we run.

Trace the word "two". Say the word "two" aloud.

two two two two two

In each sentence below, trace the word: "**two**".

Two boys are playing.

The two boys run and play.

Two apples are in the basket.

Two boys will eat the apples.

Are there two apples?

Yes. There are two apples.

Write your own sentence using the word: **two**

Read the sentences below. Circle the word "two" in each sentence. Colour the picture below.

Two boys are playing in the yard
The two boys run and play.
Two apples are in the basket.
Two boys will eat the apples.
Are there two apples?
Yes. There are two apples.

Trace the word "away". Say the word "away" aloud.

away away away

 In each sentence below, trace the word: "**away**".

The boy ran away from the bear.

The thief ran away from the policeman.

The boy ran away from the policeman.

 Write your own sentence using the word: **away**

Read the sentences below. Circle the word "away" in each sentence. Colour the picture below.

The boy ran away from the bear.

The thief ran away from the policeman.

The boy ran away from the policeman.

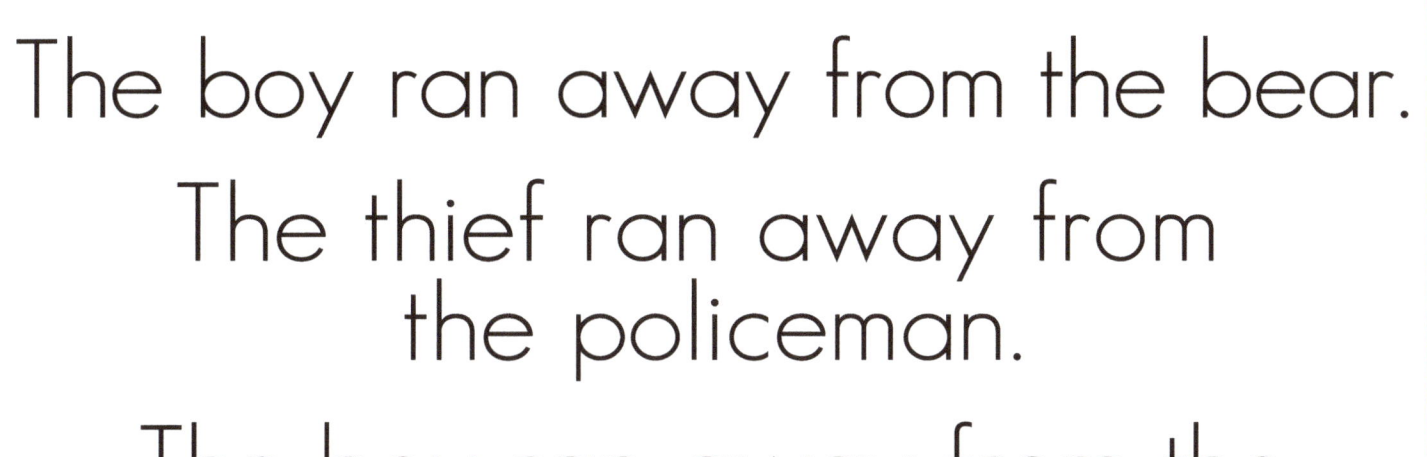

Trace the word "blue". Say the word "blue" aloud.

blue blue blue blue

 **In each sentence below, trace the word: "blue".**

The sky is blue.

The sun shines in the blue sky.

My shirt is blue.

Blue is my favourite colour.

My sister has a blue dress.

Bob has a blue bag.

 **Write your own sentence using the word: blue**

Read the sentences below. Circle the word "blue" in each sentence. Colour the picture below.

The sky is blue.
The sun shines in the blue sky.
My shirt is blue.
Blue is my favourite colour.
My sister has a blue dress.
Bob has a blue bag.

Trace the word "come". Say the word "come" aloud.

come come come

In each sentence below, trace the word: "come".

Come and see the rabbit.

Come see the bird.

You can come home with me.

Mom will come if you call.

Come and see the alligator.

Come see the deer.

Write your own sentence using the word: come

Read the sentences below. Circle the word "come" in each sentence. Colour the picture below.

Come and see the rabbit
Come see the bird in the cage.
You can come home with me.
Mom will come if you call.
Come and see the alligator.
Come see the deer.

Trace the word "down". Say the word "down" aloud.

down down down

In each sentence below, trace the word: "**down**".

Can you go down the stairs?

We go up and down.

It is fun going down the stairs.

Bob can walk down the stairs.

The children run down the stairs.

Write your own sentence using the word: **down**

Read the sentences below. Circle the word "down" in each sentence. Colour the picture below.

Can you go down the stairs?
We go up and down.
It is fun going down the stairs.
Bob can walk down the stairs.
The children run down the stairs.

Fill in the missing letters in the sight words below. Write the word correctly in the space provided then pronounce each word.

1. g ___   _____ go
2. f ___ r   _____ for
3. b ___ g   _____ big
4. c ___ n   _____ can
5. n ___ t   _____ not
6. ___ n ___   _____ one
7. r ___ d   _____ red
8. r ___ n   _____ run
9. tw ___   _____ two
10. ___ w ___ y   _____ away
11. bl ___ e   _____ blue
12. com ___   _____ come
13. d ___ w ___   _____ down

Find the words in the puzzle.

r	t	b	l	u	e	y	c
u	w	q	d	w	x	e	a
n	o	f	a	w	a	y	n
q	r	o	r	u	b	i	g
g	w	r	c	r	e	d	c
o	d	n	o	d	o	w	n
w	f	o	m	a	t	x	o
t	d	t	e	n	o	n	e

1. go
2. for
3. big
4. can
5. not
6. one
7. red
8. run
9. two
10. away
11. blue
12. come
13. down

Conduct sight word test after students have been exposed to the first fourteen sight words. Words that were incorrectly recognized should be reviewed.

SIGHT WORD TEST 2

Date: _____

Name: _____
Administrator: _____

SIGHT WORDS	PRE TEST	POST TEST	POST TEST
go			
for			
big			
can			
not			
one			
red			
run			
two			
away			
blue			
come			
down			
PERCENTAGE			
Total Correct	/13	/13	/13

Flash cards: Cut cards and paste them on cartridge paper or cardboard. Allow students to use these cards in board games and matching activities to help in memorizing words.

go	for
big	can
not	one
red	run
two	away
blue	come
	down

www.ingramcontent.com/pod-product-compliance
Lightning Source LLC
Chambersburg PA
CBHW041227040426
42444CB00002B/80